She was called Sheena.

3

She took Dad's tie.

She put it in a bag.

She took Mum's ear-ring.

She put it in the bag.

She took Dad's watch.

The children went to a show.

Mum and Dad took them.

A conjuror was in the show.

She put it in the bag.

She took Dad on to the stage.

She put the bag on Dad's head.

Sheena took a big box.

She put Wilma inside.

Sheena took her wand.

'Hey presto!' she said.

'Hey presto!' said Wilma.